The River Amazon is the longest river in South America, and one of the longest rivers on the planet.

As the River Amazon is not just one river but many small streams that join together, it is difficult to know exactly how long it is.

The River Amazon starts in the Andes Mountains in Peru. From there, it flows across to Brazil, and then into the Atlantic. By the time the river reaches Brazil, it is so big that it can be seen from space without a telescope!

There are only a few small towns and villages scattered along the river and in the surrounding rainforest. However, the huge and modern Brazilian city of Manaus sits close to it, in the middle of the Amazon rainforest.

Huge rainforests surround the River Amazon. It is rainy, hot, and humid in these rainforests. Every year in the rainy season, parts of the river rise more than 30 feet (9m). That is about as tall as two houses! The river overflows onto the land and forest around it.

river overflow

Spanish and Portuguese explorers, called conquistadors, sailed to South America from the fourteen to the sixteen hundreds intending to conquer it, and looking for gold and other riches to steal and take back with them.

Francisco de Orellana explored the river in 1542 (fifteen forty-two). Orellana was looking for cinnamon trees. The bark of the cinnamon tree was used as a spice in cooking and was very expensive.

After the conquistadors had invaded the tribes' land, they were in turn attacked by male and female fighters who were trying to defend themselves and property. It is said that the female fighters made the conquistadors think of the Greek legend of the Amazons, a tribe of female fighters led by a queen, and that is why they called the place Amazonia.

Francisco de Orellana and the conquistadors

Sadly, the conquistadors carried diseases, such as measles and smallpox. As the native tribes had not had these diseases before, many of them died. Sometimes, whole tribes died at once.

Today, there are around 400 different tribes living in the rainforests alongside the Amazon river. Most tribes are very small and live in remote places deep in the forest, where they get all they need to survive. Some tribes settle by the river and do not travel around. Other tribes have had no contact with other tribes or modern people.

Some tribes live in villages, building houses and growing crops. Others live nomadic lives deep in the forest. They roam around to find food and make temporary shelters to live in. They hunt using blowpipes, bows, and arrows.

Some arrows have poison on the tips. Poison is made from leaves, roots, and animals such as frogs that live in the forest.

There are lots of insects in the Amazon rainforest. To protect themselves from being bitten, the Amazonian people rub themselves with clay, or use vegetable oils that repel insects. Some of these oils are now used to make modern insect repellents.

Oils and dyes are sometimes also used as face paint. Different tribes have different patterns.

Many of the Amazonian tribes make jewelry and headdresses from the leaves and animals around them. The Tembe tribe make headdresses from the feathers of macaw parrots.

The Tembe are a settled tribe and their children go to school. At school they are also told about the threats to where they live and their way of life. Their villages are a mix of the old and the modern. As well as bows and arrows, they have TVs and phones.

Despite living there for hundreds of years, many of the Amazonian tribes do not own the land they live on. Over time, outsiders have taken the land and tried to force the tribes out, or even kill them. Efforts are now being made, however, to help tribes, and to stop others stealing or destroying the places where they live.

Today, Amazonian tribes and the rainforests they live in also face another threat. Large patches of forest have been burned down so that the land can be used for grazing cattle or to get other valuable resources.

burned patch of rainforest

The trees in rainforests are important to everyone. They absorb huge amounts of carbon dioxide from the air (a gas that can heat up the Earth), and release oxygen into it (the gas that we breathe).

The rainforest is huge. Hundreds and thousands of different types of trees, animals, and insects live there. Some we already know about but there are many more that have not been found yet.

The capybara is the largest rodent, and is a close relative of the guinea pig. Capybaras have webbed feet, which help them to swim.

The Amazon is also home to piranhas. These fish have a row of sharp teeth which interlock and have a very strong bite. Generally, piranhas are not as savage as you might think.

piranhas

The native tribes eat piranhas, and use piranha teeth as tools for hair cutting, arrow sharpening, and wood carving.

Anaconda snakes live in the shallow edges of the river. They sit with just their nostrils showing, waiting for an animal to go by.

Anacondas are constrictors. To constrict means to squeeze, and anacondas coil their body around and around their catch before squeezing it. When it is dead, the anaconda stretches its mouth open and eats the animal whole. It can even eat a capybara!

The manatee, or giant sea cow, has thick, wrinkled skin and long whiskers. They are related to elephants and have a large flexible upper lip. They usually live alone. They swim along the bottom of the riverbed and use their flippers to dig up weeds and roots.

Sadly, manatees have been hunted a lot. So much so, that there are not many left and they have been added to a list of animals that are in danger of becoming extinct.

At certain times, the flow of the Amazon river reverses, and goes upstream instead of down to the sea. During the extra high spring tides, this makes a giant tidal wave called the Pororoca, which can be as high as 13 feet (4m). A surfing event is held each year for this reason.

In 2003, a Brazilian man called Picuruta Salazar rode a wave for 12.5km (7.8 miles), which took him 37 minutes.